People FIRST

*"An Easy & Proven Way to Build
Profitable Business!"*

UNLOCKING the Potential
of Your Greatest Asset *in BUSINESS*

People FIRST

PREETI GUREJA

India's Leading Culture Coach & Creator of ASTHA Framework

Worldwide Published by
Pendown Press

PENDOWN PRESS LLP

An ISO 9001 & ISO 14001 Certified Co.,

Regd. Office: 3767A, Kanhaiya Nagar,

Tri Nagar, Delhi-110035

Ph.: 8180886000, 9650072927, 8595249536

E-mail: info@pendownpress.com

Branch Office: 1A/2A, 20, Hari Sadan, Ansari Road,

Daryaganj, New Delhi-110002

Ph.: 011-45794768

Website: PendownPress.com

First Edition: 2023

Price: ₹259/-

ISBN: 978-93-5554-753-8

Layout and Cover Designed by Pendown Graphics Team

Printed and Bound in India by Thomson Press India Ltd.

I dedicate this book to:

Every business owner, stakeholder, and leader who tirelessly guides and nurture their teams, understanding that the heart of every organisation beats with the people who compose it.

To My Mentor, Mr Sunil Rawat and my Marketing Guru, Akshar Yadav.

And especially to my biggest support my better half Surjeet & my son Jeevan. My family has been my biggest source of encouragement in this journey. Your unwavering support has been my driving force.

Thank you for being the pillars of strength and inspiration in my life.

This book is dedicated to all of you, with heartfelt gratitude and deep appreciation.

Contents

Preface

"Every organisation is built on the harmonious integration of three core attributes:

Technology, which empowers efficiency and innovation;

Processes, which provide structure & and consistency

People, who bring creativity, dedication and business to the organisation."

People are the heartbeat of every organisation. They are not just employees with job titles and responsibilities; they are the architects of innovation, the drivers of growth, and the source of a company's unique identity.

When we put **"People First"** in our businesses, we unlock a world of untapped potential and set the stage for extraordinary success.

This book is a testament to the power of prioritizing people in business. It is a journey through the essential principles, strategies, and stories that illustrate the transformative impact of embracing a people-first approach. It explores how organisations that invest in their employee's well-being, growth, and fulfilment not only grow but also shape a more compassionate, sustainable, and prosperous future.

As the world of work continues to change at a rapid pace, with technological advancements and global challenges reshaping industries, the role of people becomes more critical than ever. It's no longer enough to view employees as mere cogs in the machine. Instead, they must be regarded as invaluable partners in achieving organisational goals and driving innovation.

This book takes into various aspects of the People First approach. We'll explore the importance of a winning culture, trust, empathy, and open communication, and how these qualities can lead to stronger teams and more engaged teams.

We'll also discuss the role of leadership in championing this philosophy, as well as practical strategies for implementing People First principles in your organization.

Putting **"People First"** is not just a business strategy; it's a philosophy that can reshape your organization's culture, drive innovation, and elevate your business to new heights.

It's a commitment to the well-being and growth of every individual who contributes to your success.

I invite you to join me in this journey of discovery, as we unlock the full potential of your greatest asset in business: People First.

"Businesses are as productive as their people!"

~Preeti Gureja

~1~

People First

Behind every balance sheet, every product launch, and every innovation, there are individuals whose passion, creativity, and dedication fuel the engine of progress.

"Let's imagine a company where everyone shines bright. They're not just part of the company; they are the heart of its success. When you step into this workplace or join a meeting, you can feel the positivity. People work together, come up with new ideas, and share a common purpose.

Now, imagine this as your workplace. It is a place where people matter, where their ideas are welcome, and their growth is supported. Or is it a place where employees feel like they're just doing a job, not really connected to the company's goals, and not excited about their work?

It's the collective values, beliefs, and behaviours that define how things get done. Just as individuals are the heart of a company's success. Culture is the backbone that strengthens the Organisation as a whole.

Let's start by exploring the significance of culture in shaping the destiny of businesses. We'll uncover how a culture that aligns with the 'People First' ethos isn't just a nice-to-have; it's a strategic imperative. Culture influences every facet of an organisation, from employee engagement and retention to innovation and adaptability in a rapidly changing world.

Join me as we begin this journey of transformation— a journey that starts with a simple yet profound shift in perspective: Putting People First.

"Your Culture is Your Brand."

~Preeti Gureja

~2~

Brand & Culture:
The Invisible Connection

What is a company brand? This seems to be a simple question, right?

Although, it's not that simple.

A brand is just not about a product, it's beyond its logo, it's much more than its identity.

"A brand is not what you say it is. It's what your people and you build together."

The above quote states the understanding that a brand is shaped by the real interactions and relationships the stakeholders form with its clients and customers- the value and care they add.

The brand's essence and perception are not only shaped by marketing messages or declarations. Yet these play a very important role in the Digital Era today, which helps to attract the right talent to your organisation.

In the highly competitive world today, every product and market seems to be commoditized. Trust becomes an important factor to bet on.

When a business builds a reputation as an excellent product/service trusted provider, the impression it makes on customers is its brand.

Trust grows as the company regularly meets or exceeds expectations.

What is a culture? Is it easy or hard to change the culture of the organisation?

These days, leaders often say they want their culture more agile, and more respectful which helps them grow and prosper.

Culture is not something that can be just said or that can be conveyed just through a context. It is something that evolves every day with each one in the organisation. A leader is not only heard but also observed for every little action.

How does culture help in creating a brand?

A company whose customers are happy earns loyalty and respect by valuing their needs and caring for them. A winning culture delivers that kind of brand.

As brand expert, Denise Lee explains.

"Building a unique culture goes beyond internal aspirations. Companies that do this well also identify a desired brand identity—how you want your organisation to be perceived and experienced by customers and other external stakeholders.

How do we begin with creating culture?

The initial thing to have is absolute clarity of the goal. That is your dream culture definition for your organisation. A set of values that are a must.

Similar to the set of values that we have for our family, absolutely non-negotiable yet open-minded, innovative, forgiving, and growing. Once you have this set of desires clearly mentioned with the priorities, you can apply the **ASTHA framework** of leadership, the framework for the smallest to biggest organisation.

I'll be sharing insights on these important pillars for every organisation that is looking for culture change.

We'll also dive into the real-time case studies of some outstanding performer organisations for better understanding.

*"People Don't Buy Goods and Services;
They Buy Relations, Stories, and Magic."*

~Seth Godin

~3~

The Powerful Frame Work
of Leadership: ASTHA

Attraction

The apt organisational process starts with attracting the right people to fit in your organisation. Effective and attractive, magnetic branding is the key component of the First Element ATTRACTION.

Selection

Identifying the right candidate, who possesses the required job role skills is important, although willingness to learn and grow within the organisation is a must.

Transition

The first impression is the last impression; Transition of new joiners is their first stage in your organisation. It has to be the best, to showcase the behaviours, values, beliefs, and culture at your organisation.

Holistic Advancement

It's time to get back to the basics for advancement, A candidate not only looks for the pay cheques but also for continuous professional & personal growth, career progression, and all that contributes to their success.

Attrition

It's part of every business, it helps us understand how great the - is at retaining top talent over a period of time other than increased salaries.

Your people are not listening to what you say, but what you do. Because your leadership team is the one by which the entire organisation is influenced and seen as a role model.

ASTHA is a powerful framework that can be used in any and every organisation that has a strength of more than 2.

Let's explore and understand each element in detail with amazing stories.

*"Your people are your brand ambassadors,
representing your values and essence
to the world, choose them wisely."*

~Preeti Gureja

~4~

Attraction: Be Magnetic!

With a rise in flexible work environments with flexible schedules, candidates are driven by incentives and innovation. Attracting top talent becomes a challenge.

Today, from having a defined company culture to engaging with customers and followers on social media, there are many ways to grab the interest of the right candidates.

A candidate would research, and follow the message that your brand shares in social media. It is important to give a consistent message to the market of WHY the brand exists. What are the beliefs and value system that makes the life of people Happy, sustainable, and attractive?

Candidates who align with your values and business purpose will be more likely to apply to your open positions if you create a message that's well-known and consistently expressed and marketed well.

"Jo dikhta hai wohi bikta hai"

Your brand is your business's "personality"

Is recruitment, the job of a recruiter only?

Let's hear from the experts,

Dan Hoyle, brand Marketing at LinkedIn in his article on LinkedIn writes about the Reimagined Recruiter-Hiring Manager Relationship. Let's dive into this and see how Netflix actually does this.

Recruiters and hiring managers work together all the time, but that doesn't mean they're really collaborating. Instead, it can often feel like a vendor-customer relationship: managers place orders, and recruiters fill them by following predefined processes. Sure, there are discussions and adjustments, but it's ultimately more about tactics (A particular method used to achieve something) than strategy.

But not at Netflix. Just like the streaming service reinvented the way we watch movies, **they've totally reimagined the relationship between recruiters and managers as a real consultative partnership, rather than transactional order-taking.**

This is the centrepiece of Netflix's "culture of recruiting," where finding and hiring talent is everyone's responsibility.

What makes Netflix's culture different: **Everyone is responsible for recruiting.**

Netflix recruiter Chrissy Running notes that "the relationship between recruiter and hiring manager here, I think, is one of a kind." Hiring manager Chris Saint-Amant agrees: "What's really unique about the culture around recruiting at Netflix is the collaboration between the hiring manager and the recruiting team," he says.

This unique partnership stems from an overarching culture of recruiting that extends beyond the talent acquisition team and hiring managers. Everyone knows that hiring is a top priority, and that directive inspires a different kind of collaboration.

"When there's that mindset that hiring is a top priority, you really value the partnership that you have with your recruiters," says Chrissy. **"I think recruiting at other companies can be very tactical or operational, and what I love here is that it's very consultative and strategic."**

Rather than a removed, mechanical effort where recruiters follow prescribed processes—" sitting behind a desk and sending [hiring managers] resumes," as Chrissy puts it—the two truly work together every step of the way. "When there's more to the relationship than just tactical logistics going back and forth, it adds more value," she says. This sort of relationship is way more dynamic, energizing both recruiters and hiring managers.

The three elements that make Netflix's culture unique, with takeaways on how you can cultivate the same kind of relationships.

1. **Freedom:** Hiring managers have more freedom and ownership over hiring decisions.

2. **Candor:** Recruiters and hiring managers communicate directly and honestly

3. Empathy: Hiring managers and recruiters genuinely care about each other's success

So Here Are Some Techniques To Improve Your Hiring Strategy And Help You Attract The Right Talent:

1. Clearly define every position and its responsibilities

2. Determine the time frame for hiring a position and stick to It

3. Be Prompt

4. Calculate the anticipated cost and benefit for each position

5. Leverage employee referrals and recommendations

6. Get everyone interested in hiring

7. Review & update hiring strategies periodically to reflect changes.

*"Build your people
and they'll build your business."*

~Preeti Gureja

~5~

One Bad Apple
Can Cost You Lakhs!

WHY is it Important to select the right candidate, for the right position?

Selecting the right fit is an important process because a candidate or a good resource can become an asset to an organisation and increase the overall performance of the organisation.

On the other hand, if there is a bad hire with a bad selection process, it can not only backfire but also spoil the entire culture of an organisation.

Every organisation has its own criteria to select the right fit.

The cost of a bad hire in India:

Shockingly India stands at number 4 in the world when weighing companies that make wrong hiring decisions.

Believe it or not, an average of over **INR 20 Lakhs** is the cost of a bad hire.

This includes-

- Cost of hiring

- Cost of training

- Cost of productivity loss

- Cost of motivation loss

- Cost of reputation loss

One bad apple can spoil the entire barrel!

As detailed in the LinkedIn article written by me, BAD IS STRONGER THAN GOOD!!!

Toxic Employees destroy your culture and your bottom line, proves a Harvard Research.

Feelings of mistrust can destroy a culture faster than anything else.

Toxic damage cannot be contained if leaders wait too long.

Even in the happiest organisations, unhappy people can wreak havoc. It takes only one bad apple to ruin a barrel.

Toxic people alienate their co-workers and team members, which also directly impacts the bottom line, as researched by Harvard -

- 80 % of employees lost work time worrying about the offending employee's rudeness.

- 78 % said their commitment to the organisation declined in the face of toxic behaviour.

- 66 % said their performance declined.

- 63 % lost work time in avoiding the offender.

The most alarming are:

25 % of employees **who had been treated with incivility admitted to taking their frustrations out on customers and families too.**

That has a direct impact on the business.

Six Types of Toxicity Ruining Great Work Teams are:

1. Bullying

2. Causing turnover

3. The emotional messes

4. Creating destructive conflict

5. Decreasing Productivity

6. Unhappy environment

How to handle these toxic situations:

1. Simply wish the toxic people goodbye. Plus, your business can't handle that for long.

2. Address your people's complaints on the highest priority.

3. Create policies that require and reward the transfer of knowledge.

4. Absolute NO NO for Gossiping.

5. Creation of a Performance Improvement Plan; continuous learning environment for their growth.

6. Lead by example.

7. Encourage teamwork.

8. Safety is the utmost important entity that encourages our people to take ownership.

Your Teams can either make or break your business, and one bad apple can have a major impact.

It's important that you address toxic people as soon as possible to reduce the negative impact on your organisation.

If there's a bad hire, many times there is an underlying reason for their behaviour that can be solved.

It's always a good idea to address them with compassion and empathy, with the goal of finding a solution that benefits everyone.

"When WHY is Clear How becomes easy."

~Preeti Gureja

~6~

The WHY

I am done, I'll stop… I can't write anymore... writing is such a difficult task; I was really tired... couldn't think of much to start afresh with...

Okay, stop! said Jeevan, my 11-year-old boy.

Mum, can I ask you something; Will you answer my question?

Yeah sure, go on…

He asked, why did you start writing? Did anyone ask you to write?

No, No one.

He asked again; why did you start writing then?

I noticed there is a special place, a dedicated rack with the label "SELF HELP BOOKS" in every bookstore, but I couldn't find a separate rack for helping others or helping teams. So, I thought to write one.

I have been asked by many leaders and clients too where I speak, Preeti we have been hearing about changing the culture but how do we instill culture change in the organisation, can you share some practical to-dos?

So, I thought this would help them bring the change, to themselves and their organisation.

Are you saying you don't want to bring that value to your clients now because you are tired? Jeevan asked.

"Let's take a break and then you restart, I am sure you will."

"By that time let me get your special coffee," said Jeevan and went into the kitchen.

I asked, "Are you sure you will make it"

Yeah mum, TRUST me.

I was stunned by the conversation, was he, Jeevan, or my mother?

This gave me food for thought WHY do we start what we start?

Why did you start your business?

What is the purpose you are solving?

How THE WHY can help in building culture

- **Embrace the Power of Purpose:** When your organisation understands and embraces its "why," it becomes a guiding force that shapes the culture. Clearly communicate your purpose to your team, align their work with this higher mission, and watch as a shared sense of purpose drives engagement, collaboration, and a strong culture.

- **Cultivate Authenticity and Trust:** Building a culture rooted in "why" requires authenticity and trust. Leaders must lead by example, consistently demonstrating their belief in the organisation's purpose. Encourage open communication, transparency, and vulnerability, allowing employees to feel valued and connected to the greater mission. This fosters a culture where people can bring their whole selves to work, resulting in higher employee satisfaction and a strong sense of belonging.

- **Connect Actions to Values:** To build a culture that embodies the "why," ensure that your organisation's values are clearly defined and integrated into daily practices. Encourage employees to align their actions with these values, reinforcing the purpose-driven culture. Celebrate and recognize individuals and teams that exemplify the values, reinforcing their importance and inspiring others to follow suit.

"It's not about what goes in,
it's about what comes out.
A cow eats grass and gives milk,
and A Snake drinks milk and gives poison.
Words have power. Use them wisely
irrespective of the situation."

~Preeti Gureja

Words Have Power

"Hey, hey, hey! Are you stupid?

Don't you ever do that again?"

And guess what happened?

He did it again.

I have a son who is four, and he had this bad habit of writing on the walls with crayons. One evening I walked into his room and he was going at it, just writing and drawing and so on.

Whether discouraging or encouraging words have POWER.

A simple choice of 'word' can make a difference between someone accepting or denying your message. You can have a very beautiful thing to say, but say it in the wrong words and it's gone

Nobody likes to be threatened. Nobody likes to be intimidated. His pride will not allow it. He did it again just to spite me. A week later, I walked into his room and again, he was going at it and this time, he was even looking at me, just. I came down, I said "Sweetie, come here. Don't do that, you're a big boy now." And he never did it again, because his pride wants him to be 'the big boy'.

Above are the famous lines by Toastmasters world champion, **Mohammed Qahtani.**

Words have energy and power with the ability to help, to heal, to hinder, to hurt, to harm, to humiliate, and to humble."

It is vital to always speak your truth, but we must be mindful of what we say and how we say it. Your words can change everything.

Let's take an instance from team Nexus:

The Nexus team was facing interpersonal conflicts and strained communication, and crucial conversations played a pivotal role in transforming their dynamics. The team consisted of individuals with diverse backgrounds and perspectives, which often led to misunderstandings and conflicts. These issues hindered collaboration, productivity, and overall team morale.

Recognizing the importance of addressing these concerns, the team members decided to engage in a series of crucial conversations. They created a safe space where everyone could express their thoughts and concerns openly and honestly.

During these conversations, team members actively practised respectful listening and sought to understand different perspectives. They focused on discussing the impact of their actions and words on others, rather than placing blame. By sharing their own experiences and emotions, they fostered empathy and connection.

As the conversations progressed, team members discovered shared goals and interests. They realized that despite their differences, they all wanted the team to succeed and create a positive work environment. This common ground became the foundation for collaboration and finding solutions to their challenges.

The team members learned to choose their words carefully, using language that was inclusive, respectful, and solution-oriented. They encouraged each other to provide constructive feedback, focusing on specific behaviours and their impact. This allowed for personal growth and improvement without damaging relationships.

Over time, these crucial conversations and series of training helped to rebuild trust among team members. They created a culture of open and honest communication, where conflicts were seen as opportunities for growth rather than threats. As a result, the team became more cohesive, collaborative, and productive.

This illustrates the transformative power of crucial conversations in resolving conflicts, restoring trust, and creating a positive team culture. It emphasizes the importance of open dialogue, active listening, and choosing words that promote understanding and unity.

Visions for Action:

To win over your team, the best thumb rule to follow is— PIP & CIP

**PIP- Praise In People
CIP- Criticize In Private**

No one likes to be scolded, yelled at or criticized, and that too publicly. Public criticism tends to trigger defensive reactions and make it much harder for a person to accept that they have made a mistake and learn from it.

Although feedback is important at times for your people's continuous improvement and learning, but with care and concern.

React or respond

Destructive words can even make a plant wilt, thank God we are humans. Immediate reaction to any situation is always destructive. Take a pause do not respond to this situation immediately.

Be responsible for your words

Speech is silver, silence is gold. Words that are positive and uplifting create an environment of positivity and growth.

"A team is not a group of people who work together. A team is a group of people who trust each other."

~Simon Sinek

~8~

TRUST- The Foundation of a Strong Brand

"We will overcome every obstacle that comes our way, together" reassured Lt Manoj.

"If we encounter heavy fire, stay calm and focused. Remember, we are a team, there for each other.

I trust each one of you, yes, each one of you!!!

"Sir, the enemy's defences seem impenetrable. How do we proceed?" asked Naik Digendra.

"We may be outnumbered and facing difficult terrain, but remember, it's our unity and trust that will give us the edge. We will flank the enemy, attack from multiple angles, and rely on each other's cover and support. Trust in one another." Said Lt Manoj.

"But the risks are immense, sir; will we make it?

"We can never be certain of the outcome, but we must have faith in our abilities and in the bond we share. Together, we are an unstoppable force. Trust in your instincts, trust in our collective strength, and we will prevail. declared Lt Manoj

During the 1999 Kargil War between India and Pakistan, the Indian Army faced a challenging situation in recapturing strategic peaks that had been infiltrated by enemy forces. One such peak was Point 4875, a formidable stronghold at a high altitude with treacherous terrain.

To reclaim Point 4875, the Indian Army's 13th Battalion of the Jammu and Kashmir Rifles, led by Lieutenant Colonel Vishwanathan, embarked on a daring mission. However, due to the difficulty of the terrain and the intense enemy fire, the initial assault was unsuccessful, resulting in the loss of many soldiers.

Undeterred by the setback, Lt. Col. Vishwanathan and his men regrouped and launched another attack. This time, a young officer, Lieutenant Manoj Kumar Pandey, took charge of leading a small team to flank the enemy position. With fierce determination and unparalleled bravery, they pushed forward, overcoming heavy resistance and eliminating enemy positions one by one.

As the assault continued, Lt. Pandey's team encountered a bunker heavily fortified with enemy soldiers. Realizing that time was of the essence, Lt. Pandey fearlessly charged ahead, single-handedly taking out the enemy soldiers and clearing the way for his comrades to advance.

In this critical moment, Lt. Pandey displayed unwavering trust in his team. Despite the overwhelming odds, he trusted that his fellow soldiers would provide covering fire and support him in his daring assault.

Their synchronized efforts and trust in one another resulted in the successful capture of Point 4875.

Tragically, Lt. Manoj Kumar Pandey lost his life during the fierce battle, but his exceptional leadership and the trust he instilled in his team left an indelible mark. His courageous actions and unwavering trust serve as a testament to the vital role trust plays in the Indian Army and any high-performing team.

This inspiring story exemplifies how trust forms the backbone of a team's success, enabling them to overcome daunting challenges and achieve extraordinary feats. It highlights the importance of leaders fostering trust within their teams, inspiring individuals to place their faith in each other, and forging unbreakable bonds that lead to collective victory.

"Embrace the power of trust to ignite a company's culture, enabling leaders to create a safe, supported, and connected environment where team members THRIVE, productivity SOARS, and revenue reaches new HEIGHTS."

The deeper question is where it comes from. And how do you go about building it?

Without trust, you can't create value, trust is the primary ingredient of any kind of relationship.

Jeff Burkhart said, "People don't leave bad jobs, they leave bad bosses" It takes trust to keep the whole team together.

Trust isn't that will come to you, it has to be earned. The way we have earned our kids and family's trust is "No matter what I am there always for you" is something that showcases trust within them.

Value and attention:

Everyone likes to feel valued at home in social circles and even at the workplace. Right from a kid to an adult. Whether she is a housemaker or a working woman.

It's imperative to give them the freedom to explore new ideas and show their creativity. We encourage our kids to learn from every failure, so why not to our team, our people?

Appreciate:

Words are appreciation, create wonders. The famous experiment that was conducted at the "Royal Horticulture Society's"kind and appreciative words towards plants made them grow an inch taller and faster. Whereas the plants were shouted and spoken negative words either wilted or had very slow growth. The experiment was conducted with plants, isn't it the same with human beings too?

Appreciating and valuing another person helps in building trust at a quick pace.

No one ever created a win-win relationship without letting the other person win first.

Listening:

The presence of disagreements means the team trusts you enough and is not afraid to tell you the truth.

Responsibility:

Take the blame, being their leader, when an undesirable outcome happens.

Being a leader, it becomes your duty to take the blame for the good of the whole team even if it's not your fault directly.

Take responsibility for every good and bad action and your team will start trusting you.

Leading:

Your people will never listen to what you speak, but learn what you do. Action speaks louder than words. If you want your team to arrive on time, make sure to be in the office on time first.

*"Culture of belonging:
Where authenticity is celebrated, diversity is
embraced, and unity is forged."*

~Preeti Gureja

~9~

Ownership - Cultivating a Culture of Belonging

A strong company Culture plays a huge role in the success of a company. Your People are the backbone of your company and play an important role in its productivity and success. You can experience a major setback if this fails.

One of the most famous leaders who took ownership of unintended effects was Johnson & Johnson's former CEO, James Burke. In 1982, the company experienced a crisis when seven people died after taking cyanide-laced Tylenol capsules from bottles that had been tampered with. It would have been easy for Johnson & Johnson to sidestep responsibility, especially since the tampering did not occur inside J&J-owned facilities. Instead, Burke immediately took control. He pulled Tylenol from the shelves, stopped advertising it, tested 8 million pills by the end of the first week of the recall, offered customers coupons to make up for the bottles they might have to throw away, and had the company design a new tamper-evident triple seal, which was adopted by other pharmaceutical companies. He spent $100 million on the recall — an overreaction.

As per experts,

Tylenol accounted for 17% of Johnson & Johnson's net income, and marketers predicted the brand would never recover but within a couple of months, Johnson & Johnson's stock regained its previous heights.

Burke's commitment to taking responsibility earned him a spot among Fortune's 10 greatest CEOs and a place in the history books. In an era when recalls were rare, Burke pioneered a new way of understanding a company's total impact and taking action when the impact was far from positive.

There is no one way for leaders to gain, regain, or keep the trust of their stakeholders, as these examples illustrate. However, CEOs and others would be wise to take each of these dimensions seriously to ensure their companies are competitive and continue to bring in a profit. Because in order to do and keep their jobs, they must have the trust of the people who own their company, work for it, and buy or use its products.

In "Dare to Lead" - Brené Brown unveils the connection between vulnerability and innovation, showing how leaders who are willing to take risks and be vulnerable create environments where creativity flourishes. She encourages leaders to cultivate resilience and address shame and fear head-on, fostering a sense of bravery that enables growth and development.

Brown's book challenges conventional notions of leadership, urging leaders to embrace empathy, vulnerability, and wholeheartedness. By doing so, she argues, leaders can create environments where individuals feel seen, heard, and valued, leading to increased trust, collaboration, and overall success.

In essence, "Dare to Lead" inspires leaders to embrace their authentic selves, step into vulnerability, and create cultures of courage and compassion, ultimately transforming organisations and empowering individuals to reach their full potential.

''The biggest communication problem is
we do not listen to understand,
we listen to reply.''

~Stephen Covey

~10~

When Communication Fails, Organisations Fail

Communication isn't just a part of life; it is life. It's the vital force that sustains our relationships, nurtures our health, fuels our businesses, and shapes the very culture we inhabit. "In our life - communication is the thread that binds everything together."

For every ailing area in a life - miscommunication has to be blamed. Miscommunication often lies at the root of numerous ailments in various aspects of our lives. Whether it is our relationships, our personal well-being, our finances or the world of commerce and marketing- it's the failure to communicate effectively that often bears the blame.

When we fall short in conveying our thoughts and feelings to our loved ones, it can erode the very foundation of our relationships, leaving them strained and fragile.

Neglecting to communicate our needs and concerns to our own bodies can lead to a decline in our health, as our bodies struggle to understand and adapt to our innermost needs.

Failing to engage with our customers results in a sharp decline in our enterprise's fortunes, potentially leading to its downfall.

Moreover, when we overlook the importance of communication within our teams, unknowingly a negative culture starts building those interrupts and declines growth.

Communication failures can happen to anyone, anytime, and anywhere. They can cause misunderstandings, conflicts, missed opportunities, and damaged relationships. Although these can be handled effectively and constructively; if we know when and how failure happens.

Communication failure can occur within a team at various stages and for a multitude of reasons— a lack of clarity, poorly defined objectives, lack of feedback, conflicts, information overload, ineffective leadership etc.

The world's biggest disaster was caused by miscommunication:

Titanic Disaster (1912): The RMS Titanic, a passenger liner, famously sank on its maiden voyage after colliding with an iceberg. Miscommunication played a significant role in the disaster, as the crew failed to adequately relay iceberg warnings to the bridge, leading to the ship's tragic collision.

The Benefits of Clear Communication

Improved communication systems can directly lead to:

- Effective teamwork

- Increase in morale and engagement

- People feel connected to a greater whole

- Greater Innovation (as ideas can be shared easily)

- Encouraging linear and people-to-people communication

If an individual's suggestion cannot be accommodated, simply responding helps people feel heard and it cultivates an environment of free-flowing ideas.

If companies can focus on these areas, they'll be on their way to creating higher engagement, and productivity and, ultimately, boosting their bottom line. So, it pays not to underestimate the importance of company communications, especially in a growing business.

How to prevent communication failure?

When sending a work message, two vital aspects are often overlooked: simplicity and relevance. Essentially, good communication can turn engaged employees into brand ambassadors and help boost the business and attract top talent.

- **Creating an extensive plan.**

   Whether you're releasing a campaign or launching a new product, it's important to have a plan that involves the entire team. Promote teamwork to identify and fix mistakes, and explain the concepts of the plan so everyone can comprehend their responsibilities.

- **Prioritize widespread communication.**

  When every member of your team fully understands the objectives, the quality of their work can increase, and your projects can resonate with your target audiences. Communicate with your team frequently and encourage conversations between departments to **clarify ideas and invite innovation to the workflow.**

- **Channelling the viewpoints of clients.**

  Contemplate your company's brand and its products or services in the same ways as your consumers. Their expectations can impact the success of your campaigns, and you can learn how to reflect their interests and needs when you interact with them.

- **Taking responsibility for our own actions.**

  If the organization makes a mistake, it's important to be transparent about what transpired and focus on how you can improve for the future.

  Showing the supporters that you value accountability and are receptive to constructive criticism.

*"Customer service should not be
a department but an attitude
to give the best."*

~Preeti Gureja

~11~

A Fresh Croissant

Customer-centricity is a business strategy that's based on putting your customer first and at the core of your business to provide a positive experience and build long-term relationships.

Culture plays a critical role in enabling customer centricity. A culture that cultivates empathy, employee empowerment, continuous improvement, and customer advocacy creates an environment where organisations can truly prioritize and serve their customers' needs effectively.

The employee-first mindset and culture will always make the company stand out.

"Look after your people, and they'll take care of your customer."

As with many business disciplines, customer-centricity is about more than systems and tools. At root, it is about cultural transformation, and successful execution ultimately depends on people. The simple truth is that you cannot expect employees to treat customers better than they themselves are treated.

Marry customer-centricity with employee engagement.

Market leaders in customer-centricity ensure the entire company keeps customers and their needs at the forefront of planning, decision-making, and day-to-day execution.

Three key practices enable them to do so:

1. Inspire and engage your people

2. Empower your people with customer insights

3. Start with Leadership

All the above three can be visualised with this amazing story by Steve Wynn, the founder of Wynn Resort & Casino, who shared a story of his family's vacation in Paris. They were staying at the Four Seasons and had ordered breakfast in bed. His daughter only ate half of a croissant, leaving the other half for later. Wynn and his family left to explore Paris, and upon returning to the hotel room, the croissant was gone. His daughter was disappointed, assuming the housekeeping had got rid of it.

On the telephone, there was a message from the front desk. They said that housekeeping had removed the half croissant from the room, assuming that upon arrival, they would prefer a fresh croissant. So, the front desk contacted the kitchen to set aside a croissant, and room service was informed that upon request, they would need to deliver the pastry.

The level of teamwork and communication between different departments in the hotel was simply magical.

All participants understood the end result – customer satisfaction.

And everyone accepted their role in making the experience fantastic.

It shows that in order to achieve satisfaction on different levels within the organization, employees should be empowered to be creative, intuitive, thorough, and generous.

Next time you offer a service or a product do recheck if it's as fresh as the Four Season croissant.

"Your feedback can ignite the fire of excellence in someone's heart and help him to reach the pinnacle. Make it count by delivering it effectively."

~Preeti Gureja

~12~

The Power of Feedback

Mary: Good morning, everyone! Thank you for joining me today. I want to express my sincere appreciation to each of you for your commitment to General Motors and for actively participating in our feedback system. Your input is invaluable in helping us create a safer and more innovative workplace.

John: Good morning, Ms. Barra. Thank you for creating this opportunity to discuss important matters with you.

Mary: The pleasure is mine, and I genuinely value your presence here. We are a team, and our collective efforts shape the future of this company. Today, I want to focus on the issue of safety, which is paramount to our success. We all understand the potential consequences of overlooking safety concerns, both for our customers and our reputation.

Smith: Thank you, Ms. Barra, for highlighting the significance of safety. It's a responsibility we take seriously, and we appreciate your leadership in this regard.

Mary: You're most welcome, and I'm glad to hear that. Our commitment to safety extends beyond mere words—it requires action. I want to take this moment to acknowledge the exceptional work done by our team recently. By speaking up about a safety issue, you have demonstrated a deep sense of responsibility and helped us avoid potential risks.

Jack: Thank you, Ms. Barra. We felt it was our duty to report the issue, and we're glad it was addressed promptly.

Mary: I cannot emphasize enough how important it is to have employees like you who are willing to voice concerns and share feedback. It's through your dedication that we continuously improve and enhance the safety standards of our vehicles. I want to personally thank each of you for your vigilance and for being an integral part of our commitment to accountability and transparency.

Steve: We are honoured to be part of a culture that values feedback and takes decisive action. It gives us the confidence to address potential safety issues without hesitation.

Mary: And that's exactly the culture we aim to foster—a culture where every employee feels empowered to contribute and make a difference. I assure you that we will continue to support your efforts by providing the necessary resources and implementing systems to protect anonymity when reporting concerns.

Peter: That's reassuring, Ms. Barra. It encourages us to keep striving for excellence in safety and contribute to the success of General Motors.

Mary Barra: I'm glad to hear that, and I want to reiterate that your contributions are invaluable to our ongoing success.

Today, let's delve into the safety issue that has been brought to our attention and collectively work toward finding a solution that upholds our commitment to excellence and customer satisfaction.

The above conversation is of Mary Barra, CEO of General Motors and her team, who has made it a priority to build a culture of accountability and transparency at the company. She has emphasized the importance of speaking up and giving - receiving feedback, both positive and negative, she personally reached out to employees to thank them for speaking up about a safety issue, which ultimately led to a recall of millions of vehicles. Barra has also implemented a system for employees to report concerns anonymously and has taken swift action to address any issues that arise.

She embraced the participatory leadership style, where GM employees participate in the decision-making process making them feel accountable for GM's growth. Besides that, she adopted a collaborative approach and engaged employees in the decision-making process. (Jiang, 2022), however, if the consensus approach doesn't seem sufficient to make the right decision, Mary will take the consultative approach and leadership in the decision-making process. I believe that the consensus approach increases the probability of making the right decision if the involved employees are highly qualified in specific areas.

Receiving and giving feedback is one of the crucial aspects of building a good culture in any organization, including manufacturing companies. When employees feel valued and heard, they tend to be more engaged, productive, and committed to their work. On the other hand, a lack of feedback or poor feedback practices can lead to disengagement, low morale, and high turnover rates.

In manufacturing industries, it's especially important to have a culture of feedback, given the importance of safety and quality control. By encouraging open communication and feedback, employees are more likely to feel comfortable reporting safety issues or offering suggestions for process improvement.

After delving deep into the subject and interviewing many stakeholders, I've found some practical and easy-to-do's that can turn feedback into art in your company culture. These tips will not only make giving and receiving feedback a graceful experience but will also make it a crucial part of your organization's culture.

Below are a few tried & tested tips, to elevate your team's performance and take your organization to the next level.

1. Initiate the process, and ask for feedback – hear them with full attention, even if they are criticizing, you can use simple words like.. Hmm hmm OR, ok go on OR carry on OR I am all ears to you. Take action on the feedback, as you take action, your teams start believing they are being heard, they are valuable, and their opinions matter.

2. When you initiate by asking for feedback and accept it gracefully. Your people will follow you.

3. Regular feedback to the team helps to feel valued and also help them to grow., both positive and constructive.

4. Encourage the team to give feedback to each other, creating a culture of collaboration and continuous improvement.

5. Use anonymous feedback mechanisms, such as suggestion boxes or online surveys, to ensure that everyone has a voice.

6. Provide training for both managers and ICs on how to give and receive feedback effectively.

7. Transform your company into a culture of openness, trust, and growth by implementing these feedback practices. This will lead to improved employee engagement, productivity, and success.

*''When you break bread together,
you build bridges.''*

~Preeti Gureja

~13~

Chai Pe Charchaa

'*Chai pe charchaa*' - conversations over tea - bring people closer in an informal setting, and so too does the act of sharing food. It's a moment when colleagues become friends, when hierarchies fade away, and when the richness of diverse flavours mirrors the diversity of talents and perspectives in the workplace.

Food is a universal language that transcends barriers.

It doesn't matter where one comes from or what the role is; when you break bread together, you build bridges.

It creates an environment where people feel valued, heard, and connected.

And these connections fostered over food, extend beyond the dining table into the workplace, enhancing collaboration, trust, and a shared sense of purpose.

The act of sharing food isn't just about satisfying hunger; it's about nurturing relationships, fostering a sense of belonging, and binding the organisation in a way that transcends the ordinary. It's the '*chai pe charcha*' of the workplace, where the simple act of enjoying a meal together becomes a catalyst for growth, understanding, and lasting camaraderie."

Stories connect hearts and inspire minds, Stories have the power to weave the past & create inspiration & reason to be for tomorrow.

~Preeti Gureja

~14~

The Brahmastra

Brahmastra: The most powerful, divine weapon. The invincible Astra (weapon) hits its target unerringly.

People are wired to respond emotionally to the change, therefore there is something that helps them to communicate the narrative for change.

When listening to stories, our brains release oxytocin which makes audiences more compassionate.

Leaders who deliver compelling stories make them catchy, impactful, authentic, and simple.

Not only sharing stories of success but small and big failures will help, would make your people feel you are one of them, a normal human being who has earned everything and reached the pinnacle through hard work, perseverance, and dedication.

The neuroscience behind storytelling:

Humans have been telling stories for tens of thousands of years, which means our brains are hardwired to engage with the narratives we read and hear. This makes storytelling extremely effective when used with purpose and a clear direction.

How to craft a story as a business leader?

1. Why the story?

2. Message through the story.

3. Catchy

4. Knowing the audience

5. Visualising the impact

6. Authenticity is the key to good storytelling.

7. Using characters

8. Making audience hero

9. Simple stories are impactful

10. Moral and its importance.

Practice, practice, practice Cognitive psychologist Jerome Bruner suggests we are 22 times more likely to remember a fact when it has formed part of a story. So, dedicate yourself to the art of storytelling if you truly want to bring people with you.

*"Attrition: the silent departure
of talent, the hidden cost of neglecting
employee engagement."*

~Preeti Gureja

~15~

Brand Ambassadors

(With No Salary)

Attrition is inevitable, understanding why it happens and how to manage it can be a game-changer. Well, this is a common challenge - the departure of employees from an organization, is a common challenge faced by businesses.

An individual leaves any organisation mainly for any of the 3C's reasons:

1. Culture and the workplace environment (May also include bad boss)

2. Career advancement

3. Compensation

It's crucial to recognize that attrition isn't always a negative outcome; sometimes, it's a natural part of an individual's career journey.

However, what sets an organization apart is how it handles attrition.

One of the best practices in this regard is making the exit process easy and positive for departing employees. When employees leave with a good impression, it can turn them into lifelong brand ambassadors for your organization.

Think about it: A former employee who departs with a sense of respect, appreciation, and support is more likely to speak positively about your company, refer potential talent, and maintain professional connections. They become advocates for your brand, even after they've moved on.

To achieve this, taking exit interviews is a must. It's a valuable opportunity to gather feedback, understand the reasons behind attrition, and identify areas for improvement. It's a chance to part ways on good terms, leaving the door open for potential future collaborations.

Managing attrition isn't just about reducing numbers; it's about nurturing relationships. By making the exit process easy and taking exit interviews seriously, you not only foster goodwill but also gain insights that can fuel the growth and improvement of your organization.

Actually, attrition doesn't have to be the end of a relationship; it can be the beginning of a lasting connection that benefits both individuals and the organization they once called home."

Let This Not Be The End
of The Journey.....

Thank you for joining me on this transformative journey. Your commitment to the well-being of your people is not just an investment in your organization; it's a testament to the enduring spirit of humanity in the world of business.

Together, we've unlocked the potential of your greatest asset - your people paved the way for a future where they shine brightly at the forefront of your organization's success.

"The future of work is your people's well-being"

This mantra isn't just a catchy phrase; it's the essence of sustainable success in the business world of tomorrow.

Your people are the irreplaceable cornerstone of your organization's growth and prosperity. In an age where technology and automation continue to reshape industries, it's essential to remember that the machines, algorithms, and innovations we embrace remain tools to be run by human hands and guided by human minds.

I wish you all the best for the success of your organisation, where teamwork prospers, and individuals can shine.

But the journey doesn't end here; it's merely the beginning of a profound transformation.

Now, I invite you to take action and apply the insights and strategies you've discovered within these pages. The future of work is in your hands, and it starts with your people.

I would like to invite you to check the culture of your organisation. Please click the link below:

http://bit.ly/3ZJl3un

Let's connect on LinkedIn:

https://www.linkedin.com/in/
preeti-gureja-%F0%9F%8F%86-29b80917/

Email us at: preeti.gureja@learn360.co.in

Visit us at: www.learn360.co.in

Together, we can shape a future where organizations flourish, and people are at the heart of every success story.

Don't miss to take the free health check of your organization by clicking the link above and taking the first step toward a brighter future.

With heartfelt gratitude and best wishes,

~Preeti Gureja

References

https://blog.culturewise.com/company-culture-brand-image

https://www.4cornerresources.com/blog/effective-hiring-strategy/

https://www.uschamber.com/co/run/human-resources/
attracting-employees-to-your-business

7 Things Netflix Recruiters Do to Create a True Partnership With Hiring Managers (linkedin.com)

https://www.lifehack.org/411479/
your-words-have-power-use-them-wisely

https://www.successconsciousness.com/blog/success/build-trust-within-your-team/ Article by Lisa Smith.

https://hbr.org/2019/07/leading-with-trust

https://www.linkedin.com/advice/0/
how-do-you-handle-communication-failures

https://grasshopper.com/blog/8-epic-failures-of-communication/

https://www.forbes.com/sites/forbesbusinesscouncil/2022/09/08/
most-companies-internal-comms-are-broken-heres-how-to-fix-it/?sh=7d4e133d5002

https://www.indeed.com/career-advice/career-development/
communication-failure-example

https://myconnect-gocomms.rrd.com/movie/a-fresh-croissant/

https://cmr.berkeley.edu/2021/09/
what-is-customer-centricity-and-why-does-it-matter/